Skookum Book's Charms!

The beautiful butterfly, that graces our flowers and bushes, goes through a mysterious and magical change in becoming an adult! The Greeks believed each time a butterfly emerges from its cocoon, a new human soul is born! Legend has it that whispering a wish to a butterfly, then releasing it to carry the message to heaven, the wish will come true! Perhaps this is when they acquire little clouds on their wings. The butterfly is a symbol of fresh life, happiness, and joy! The night butterfly, the moth, is attracted to a flame and light, just like our souls are attracted to heavenly truths!

Hummingbirds are active, beautiful additions to our gardens, who give us a sense of life, nature's beauty, and fresh life! These "flying jewels" flit from flower to flower picking up and delivering pollen, so that life can continue. It's the creature that opens the heart and shows the truth of beauty! It brings laughter and enjoyment and the magic of being alive. The hummingbird stands for spreading love!

Copyright c 2015 by Betty Lou Rogers 41372724

All rights reserved

ISBN- 13 978-0692795187   (Skookum Books)
ISBN- 10 0692795189

All rights reserved. No part of this publication may be reproduced in any means,

In any way, without permission in writing from the copyright Owner.

With God, All Things Are Possible

Dedication: This book is dedicated to truth and honesty. This subject has gained its prominence because of the conduct of our politicians. Selfish ambition, dishonesty and untruthfulness are not the standards, for our country our founders had in mind! They had many problems to solve, but they did work together, putting the good of our nation first.

ACKNOWLEDGEMENTS

Being a parent is, no doubt, the most important job anyone can ever have. Being a good parent is probably the hardest job. I would like to acknowledge the many good parents who are dedicated to teaching their children true values and standards, and have the courage and stamina to see it through!

It's So Important To Be Honest

Betty Lou Rogers

It's so important to be honest,
You only get one chance to show,
That when you do make a statement,
It's as true as you possibly know!

It's so important to be honest,
It only takes one time to err,
If you tell only one, only one little lie,
From then on, your friends will beware!

It only takes one untrue story
To cause others to doubt what you say,
They'll always 'remember' that falsehood,
And you'll never 'forget' your disgrace!

At times you could really be tempted
To change what you know to be true,
A lie might boost your importance,
Don't do it! It only damages you!

It's so very important to be honest,
If you ever slip up just one time,
For one lie is as bad as a hundred,
And you'll regret it the rest of your life!

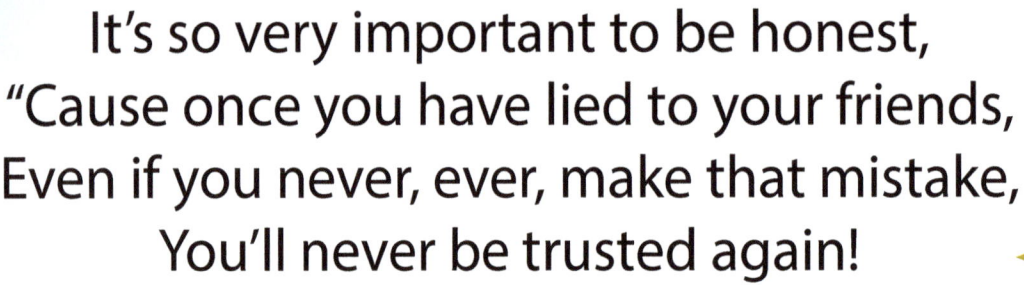

It's so very important to be honest,
"Cause once you have lied to your friends,
Even if you never, ever, make that mistake,
You'll never be trusted again!

Now, lying is thought of as cheating,
There's nothing worse than a fraud,
You'll never be looked at with value,
You'll always be thought of as flawed!

It's oh, so very important to be honest,
No one ever succeeds telling lies,
They might accumulate wealth and fame,
Which will rot, and erode, and decay with their name!

When people find you're untruthful,
Your comments mean nothing at all,
For they don't know when you 'are' honest,
So your importance, to them, is quite small!

As you become known as a liar,
To your words others won't even listen,
They're aware of your past and your cheating,
And your bad, ugly human condition!

When you are known as a liar,
People won't believe anything you say,
They remember all your false statements,
Which have caused your personal disgrace!

And for those who become accomplished liars,
They need skills to remember their words,
'Cause it's easier to recall what really happens,
Than to recollect made-up and invented concerns!

The people who deal in many lies,
Seek to conceal the truth all around,
But they never can bury it deep enough,
That it can't be dug up and found!

Are you afraid of what's truthful?
Or, can you face up to what's real?
Are you willing to change your perceptions?
About evil, and accept love which will heal!

Don't you be afraid of what's truthful,
Don't you be afraid of what's right,
Don't be afraid to change your thinking,
It's far better to correct wrongs, and unite!

It's very essential to be honest,
This should be the message you send,
For honesty is the best policy,
On this standard, everyone can depend!

So many people fear the truth,
Because it shows their thinking is wrong,
And they don't want to hear the real story,
So they blame and excuse evil, right along!

A few people don't want to hear what's truthful,
It might differ from what they've been taught,
They don't want to find they've been mistaken,
They don't want to change their actions and thoughts!

So, if you are always so honest,
And if you stay true to the truth,
Not one person ever will doubt you'
And you'll be a satisfied youth!

If ever you find it a question,
To lie or remain with what's true,
Be sure to protect your good honor,
By respecting goodness and truth!

It's so very important to be honest,
For it's one of the people's good rules,
It bolsters the goodness of living,
It's the excellence of life all should choose!

It's so very important to be honest,
Don't ever toy with the truth,
You'll find great rewards for your person,
And you'll feel, oh so much, gratitude!

Winning is wonderful, it's lots of fun,
it makes us feel, oh, so proud,
With hard work, winning's beyond compare,
But only if you've won it, playing fair and square!

Winners respect their fellow man,
They are gracious and thankful for life,
Winners don't boast, or brag, or tease,
They're truthful and honest and aim to please!

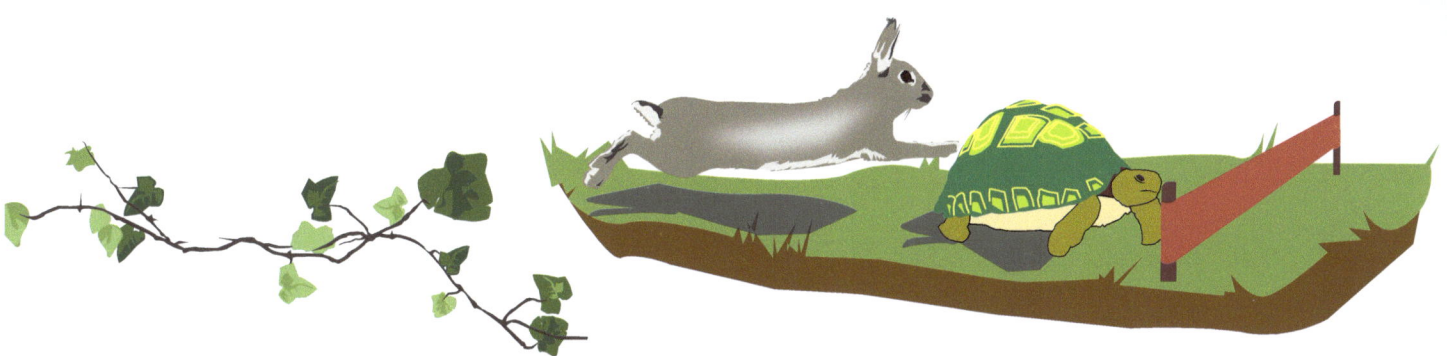

Don't be a cheater, it's the lowest to go,
You might think it's the only way to "win",
But cheating is lying, it's stealing as well,
With this kind of behavior, you'll never excel!

When you cheat, you really haven't won,
You've stolen the prize from another,
So, you cannot feel that you are the best,
Since you lied before God, and all the rest!

If you do something wrong, it's but one wrong,
If you lie about it, that makes two,
If you try to hide it, and blame someone else,
That makes four wrongs, all due to you!

Hating absolutely does no good,
And it destroys the person who hates,
The hater is filled with lies and untruths,
Those vices will produce an unhappy youth!

Honorable is when you refuse to accept,
Those who are cheating and don't tell the truth,
It is better to leave them, they only cause strife,
And go on and give yourself, to goodness in life!

A person is only as good as their word,
if you say that you're honest, then be it,
If you make a promise, then keep it,
If you stand for truth, then show it!

When you see something that's really wrong,
And others ignore it, and turn away?
Will you too, turn your back and look to the side,
Or will you fight wickedness and lies everytime?

Do you ever think, when you're gone from this earth,
Of what people are liable to say?
Will they feel they've been lucky, having known you?
Will it be for the many good deeds that you do?

Some people think they're above the law,
They think they are better than others,
Better in looks, talking, or wealth?
Probably, better in thieving and stealth!

Would you be the one, to keep our country free?
Would you fight all those, who lie and disagree?
Will you stand for goodness, truth, and honesty?
Would you live for righteousness, and do it earnestly?

And what a wonderful, rich feeling, you'll have
When you're strong, courageous, in control,
Your life's filled with goodness and passion,
And you know you're fulfilling your role!

You might take notice of some elders,
Who 'play' with the truth, when they speak,
You can be judge, jury, and commander,
And remind them, it's 'honesty' you seek!

Now, history is a true story,
It's message cannot be changed,
There are people who want to ignore that,
And tell their own version, rearranged!

It's utterly important to be honest,
It's one rule, out of "The Ten",
Moses brought them down to his people,
They're called "Ten Commandments", Amen!

If you want to make others feel worthy,
And show them you really do care,
Just light up your face, with a sunny smile,
And send friendly greetings, everywhere!

Now, when you grow weary, and full of doubt,
You want to be someone worth noting,
So, what do you do, when you feel so defeated?
"Treat others the way you'd like to be treated!"

And always remember, Never forget!

America is your homeland,
'Twas won with blood and strife,
And cherish all your freedoms.
And guard them with your life!

About the Author

Betty Lou Rogers is a retired fourth grade teacher from Madison Elementary School in Sandusky, Ohio. Her strategy for success was simple. Engage! Work Togeth! Be active learners! Then employ her "one more chance" philosophy.

Betty Lou Rogers grew up in rural northwestern Ohio, graduating from Fremont Ross High School. She married her childhood sweetheart and raised three sons. During this time, she returned to college where she graduated with a B.S. Degree in Elementary Education from Bowling Green State University in Bowling Green, Ohio. She was a member of the prestigious educational society, Kappa Delta PI.

While teaching at Madiscon School, Mrs. Rogers was keenly aware of what children needed, both as a group and as individuals, in effectual learning in the classroom. She also had the intuition to know how to accomplish this by challenging her students to be active learners, as opposed to the sit, listen, and absorb approach! Always have lesson material in front of the student, so they are actively participating in the lesson, while never pushing the child beyond their ability, but always working toward the best they can do. Often times the student is awakened to and surprised at their own ability. Mrs. Rogers' most telling educational approach was offering the children "one more chance" to succeed, by giving open-book tests! Tests show what the student doesn't know. "My job is to give the children every opportunity to learn." This strategy caused her students to become more familiar with the contents and location of information. This offering, enabled them to find the answer, complete the test, and learning what was missed before. These answers could even be more meaningful to them. When parents found this out, there was no excuse for a failing grade!

Mrs. Rogers was also a Jennings Scholar, which honored and rewarded teachers in the elementary classroom. The Jennings Foundation provides a means for greater accomplishment, on the part of teachers, with the hope it would result in greater recognition for those in the teaching profession within the public school system.

Mrs. Rogers is a member of Advent United Methodist Church in Simpsonville, S.C. Besides writing, she loves sewing and gardening. Mrs. Rogers and her husband have four grand-daughters and seven great-grandchildren.

After twenty-seven years of teaching, Mrs. Rogers philosophy for success has permeated the American landscape through her students In both academic and professional fields. Her love for teaching and writing, can never be equaled in any way, except her hope for students to find her writing truly illuminating!

Mrs. Rogers previously published works are:

The Thimseagle Thievers
Change Can Be Good!
Paste and Gluey, Sticky Tale

New publications coming are:

Kate Earns Her MBA in Manners, Behavior, Attitude
Chris Earns His MBA in Manners, Behavior, Attitude

The first in a series for teens and pre-teens.

It's So Important To Be Honest!
The Ten Comandments for Teens,
and Helpful Hints in Be-tween!
Proverbs: The First Book Written For The Young,
Plus A Little Bit For Everyone!
Acquiring The Human Skills of Thinking, Saying,
and Doing, For Teens!
A Medley of Options for the "Not Yet Old" Set!
God And Country, Two Sets of Laws For Teens!
The Human Dilemma of the Young, The Scramble for PAM!
Power, Approval, Money (Ecclesiastes)
A Hodge-Podge of Thoughts For Teens, That's Not Gibberish!
Law and Order for Teens: Ignore or Restore?
ABC's For Teens, and What They Mean!
An article that answers critics, So You Think We Shouldn't
Have Dropped "The Bomb"!

For fun: *Bossy Susie Saucy*
Capricious Caleb O'Connor

www.ingramcontent.com/pod-product-compliance
Lightning Source LLC
Chambersburg PA
CBHW041231040426

42444CB00002B/126